Abstinence Beats Recovery

A compilation of true stories provided by Alcoholics and Drug Addicts about how they got started and the consequences they have suffered. A book written to warn students of the perils of addiciton.

Let's Change the World

A process for becoming a co-worker with Christ to Change the World. Matthew 28:18-20 is your mandate to go and make Disciples of Christ of all nations and Jesus will always be with you.

Let's Change Your Church

A process for becoming a co-worker with Christ to change your church into an Obedience Driven Church. Your church's mission is to change the world.

Let's Change Your School

A process for students to become co-workers with Christ to Change their schools and start a sustained global Christian Discipleship Movement.

Let's Change You

A process for sharing Christ's yoke, to be transformed, and start a sustained, global Christian Discipleship Movement.

Let's Change Your Thinking About Sex and Marriage

How parents and the church must train children about God's reason for sex. Godly sex must be taught from early childhood through marriage.

LET'S CHANGE THE WORLD

A Process for Becoming a Co-Worker with Christ to Change the World

John and Dot Overton
Edited by: Will Overton
March 2018

www.equippingstudents.com

WESTBOW
PRESS®
A DIVISION OF THOMAS NELSON
& ZONDERVAN

Scriptures taken from the Holy Bible, New International Version®, NIV®.
Copyright © 1973, 1978, 1984, 2011 by Biblica, Inc.™ Used by permission
of Zondervan. All rights reserved worldwide. www.zondervan.com The
"NIV" and "New International Version" are trademarks registered in
the United States Patent and Trademark Office by Biblica, Inc.™

WestBow Press books may be ordered through booksellers or by contacting:

WestBow Press
A Division of Thomas Nelson & Zondervan
1663 Liberty Drive
Bloomington, IN 47403
www.westbowpress.com
1 (866) 928-1240

Because of the dynamic nature of the Internet, any web addresses or
links contained in this book may have changed since publication and
may no longer be valid. The views expressed in this work are solely those
of the author and do not necessarily reflect the views of the publisher,
and the publisher hereby disclaims any responsibility for them.

Any people depicted in stock imagery provided by Getty Images are
models, and such images are being used for illustrative purposes only.
Certain stock imagery © Getty Images.

ISBN: 978-1-9736-2611-4 (sc)
ISBN: 978-1-9736-2612-1 (e)

Library of Congress Control Number: 2018904629

Print information available on the last page.

WestBow Press rev. date: 04/19/2018

Dedication

We dedicate this book to the memory of our dear intercessor Loella Hudson.

She was our neighbor, friend, sister in Christ, and prayer partner. She was vitally interested in and supported this process. She left us on October 6, 2017 to be with Jesus.

We really miss her.

Acknowledgment

The writers were greatly influenced by Dr. Dallas Willard's trilogy, A Divine Conspiracy, The Spirit of the Disciplines, and Renovation of the Heart.

The seven checkpoints from Dr. Andy Stanley's book by that name have been used in our equipping parents and equipping students processes.

Author's Introduction

Evil seems to be winning! Nuclear bomb threats, ISIS, internal civil unrest, hatred, etc. are in each evening's news This is not God's intention. He has dwelt amongst us and commissioned us to join Him in a conspiracy to change evil to good. We are to become co-laborers with Him in this most ambitious task. He assures us that it can be accomplished.

Jesus started His Church for the purpose of making this revolutionary change but she has become irrelevant to most people today! He has provided an inspired field manual for us to use, the Bible. We must move beyond bible study and obey its commissions and commands much as a military person uses his/her field manual.

Having finished His work amongst us, Jesus empowered His disciples to continue His radical mission to change the world. This book is the writer's best effort to describe His divine plan.

God's Divine Plan: Dr. Dallas Willard has written a trilogy of books, The Divine Conspiracy, Renovation of the Heart, and The Spirit of the Disciplines, which has highly influenced the writers to prepare this process for you to become a co-conspirator with Jesus.

We have written a series of books on how Christians can transition from consumers to change agents that make radical impacts in their families, churches, schools, and the uttermost.

Matthew 28:18-20 is the major scripture that supports this conspiracy. Then Jesus came to them and said, "All authority in heaven and on earth has been given to Me. Therefore go and make disciples of all nations, baptizing them in the name of the Father and of the Son and of the Holy Spirit, and teaching them to obey everything I have commanded you. And surely I am with you always, to the very end of the age." We cite other scriptures, which builds a can-do attitude for this conspiracy.

How we fit into His plan: Following Jesus' crucifixion and resurrection, He instructed His followers to continue the work He had started. He picked men that seemed unqualified to execute His grandiose assignment. He did this so they would not attempt to change the world in their own strength. He promised to provide the spiritual resources needed to fulfill His commission.

Spiritual Disciplines are Necessary: To become a co-conspirator with Jesus, you must establish and maintain daily communion with Him. Then he said to them all: "Whoever wants to be my disciple must deny themselves and take up their cross daily and follow me" (Luke 9:23). We are told that if we will follow Him, He will make us fishers of men (Matthew 4:19). His ultimate plan is a sustained global movement to change the world and you are called to join Him in its execution.

The writers have prepared the following three-phase process for you to share Jesus' yoke and change the world. Like Jesus' disciples, you must become a co-conspirator with Him to be successful.

Phase I, Curriculum for Christlikeness, must be personally studied and applied before advancing to the second and third phases.

Phase II, Equipping Parents (EP), is the critical process for forming a team of parent disciples to launch the final phase.

Phase III, Equipping Students (ES), is the ultimate goal of this process. Students are to be equipped to take the gospel of Christ onto their campuses and start a sustained, global, discipleship movement.

The strategy for launching a sustained global Christian discipleship movement is for one or two Christian couples to equip themselves to become the managers of an ES region. You may become an ES manager by using this book to yoke yourself with Jesus to Change the World. Study and prayerfully apply the obedience assignments.

Obedience Assignment: ☐

> 1. Find a secret place away from all human sound to read this book and the Bible daily.

They are located throughout the book that follows. Check the box following your completion of each assignment. Then request to be commissioned as an ES manager / trainer by contacting us from our www. equippingstudents.com website.

All resource tools for this *Change the World* process are available for reading and downloading from our website. Pre-bound copies may be purchased at the cost of preparation and shipping. A thumb drive with all of the materials needed to prepare you and to disciple others is also available from the website.

Phase I

A Curriculum for Christlikeness

Did you locate your secret place? If not, please do not continue reading until you do.

Jesus created the world and He can change it. He intends to change it and His grand plan is for you to become a co-laborer with Him to change evil with good. You are to become His apprentice or disciple.

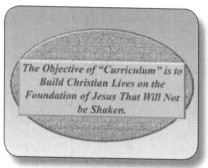

The Objective of "Curriculum" is to Build Christian Lives on the Foundation of Jesus That Will Not be Shaken.

When you try to accomplish great things in the spiritual world (His kingdom) in your own strength, you fail for lack of needed spiritual vision and power. Such self-efforts are not based on proper spiritual foundations.

Jesus clearly informs you that if you go beyond just hearing Him and obey Him, you will establish your life wisely on a solid spiritual foundation and the events of the natural world cannot shake you. He instructs you to make disciples and train them to do everything He has told you.

Those who have apprenticed themselves to Jesus enjoy an undying life with a future as good and as large as God Himself. The experiences you can have in this life as His co-conspirator can fill you with anticipation of a future so full of beauty and goodness that you can only imagine.

You may think the following curriculum is new and radical. It is radical in comparison to the current consumer Christianity being practiced, but it is not new!

This curriculum is based on the foundational tenants of real Christianity as established by Christ Himself.

Obedience Assignment: ☐

> 2. Use your secret place, be silent, and think about what heaven is like.

Apply each of these assignments in obedience to Jesus as you encounter them, and He will renew your mind (Romans 12:2). For this process to work, you must not ignore these Obedience Assignments!

Though it sounds impossible, the world system of evil and depravity can be changed if you agree it needs to be changed, and are willing to follow Jesus and practice His teachings.

"Therefore everyone who hears these words of Mine and puts them into practice is like a wise man who built his house on the rock. The rain came down, the streams rose, and the winds blew and beat against that house; yet it did not fall, because it had its foundation on the Rock" (Matthew 7:24-25).

These words from Jesus show that it must be possible to hear and do what He said. It also must be possible to train his apprentices (disciples) in such a way that they routinely do everything He said.

This will not happen if you attempt to follow His actions and commandments as if they are laws to perform.

It will happen if you undergo a renewed mind resulting in a transformation of your inner being. You will then act spontaneously rather than asking yourself, "What would Jesus do?" each time you face a decision.

Obedience Assignment: ☐

3. Keep a Bible, journal, and pen in your secret place.

Spontaneous Christlike responses may seem a dream to you today, or may be perceived as a threat to your current vision of the Christian hope. That is only because you live in a time when consumer Christianity has become the accepted norm, and all-out engagement with and in Jesus' kingdom is regarded as just one option you may take if it suits you. By contrast, the Biblical pattern is, from beginning to end, "Be ye doers of the word, and not hearers only".

His proclamation is that the kingdom of God is at hand and you are invited to enter it now rather than waiting until you die. He also assured you that all authority (power) in heaven and earth has been given to Him and He will escort you to take His gospel to the uttermost parts; thus change the world (Matthew 28:18-20). Because this is so, you now must deal with the question of ways and means for fulfilling Jesus' commission. What could you teach apprentices to Jesus, and how could you train them in such a way that they would routinely do the things He said were right? Indeed, what can you do to put yourself in a position to actually do what He has said? You already know most of what you need to know to answer the question, but now you must respond systematically with intent to obey.

It has taken two millennia to arrive at the current state of Christianity and it will take time to restore it to the kingdom Jesus so strongly proclaimed. The good news is that you and the generations to follow can begin to benefit from changes in your world now.

Christianity, as proclaimed by Jesus and His apostles, is intended to be a sustained global movement but this strategy has been lost in favor of short term benefits because of a consumer attitude. His sermon on the mount as described in Matthew 5 is all-inclusive. Current consumer Christianity too often targets people of like thinking that will support the institution.

This curriculum for Christlikeness will likely call for you to make radical changes of habits. If you are not a Christian, you will need to believe that God exists and rewards those that earnestly seek Him (Hebrews 11:6). If you are a Christian, you will need to honestly check your Christian habits against the basic gospel (Good News) incorporated in God's grand plan for you.

How God Designed You and How You Function

You may think that God created you in an unusual way. That is true but His ways are not your ways. Your great ancestors Adam and Eve were the first people that God made. The record of the creation of the earth and human beings is outlined in the first pages of the first book of the Bible: Genesis. Understanding how you and others function will help you to embark on a world-changing quest with confidence.

God created soil, water, plants, fish, birds, and animals before he made man. Man was the only being that God made in His spiritual image. God considered man special.

He deemed man as being very good! He also observed that it was not good for man to be alone - he needed a helpmate. It is important for you to know that from the beginning of time, God considered you to be special and He still does.

Too often, we establish our self-image by what we perceive other people think about us or what we think of ourselves. No matter what you or others think, God thinks that you are special and He made you for a world-scale affecting purpose. If you are seeking your purpose in life, Christianity is the way to discover it. Jesus answered, "I am the way and the truth and the life. No one comes to the Father except through me" (John14:6).

As a spiritual being, you live a spiritual life though you are presently in a physical body in a physical world. It is important to realize that Satan, who is an evil spirit here on earth, remains a defeated enemy of God, though he falsely presents himself as the way to a fun and happy life. Satan will try his very best to persuade you to follow his worldly way of life rather than God's and he does not bother to tell you that his way leads to eternal destruction (Matthew 7:13-14)!

God provided you with a temporary body to live in but the real you is an eternal, god-like soul, and spirit. He gave you five senses to interact with the physical world where you live. The sense of hearing, seeing, smelling, tasting, and feeling all feed information into your mind located in your soul.

In turn, the mind processes this information much like a computer, and informs your emotions and your will. Your will makes choices based on the processed information from the mind as filtered by your emotions. These result in actions you take into the surrounding world or culture. Thus, your mind is the core or heart of your kingdom.

This is the natural man and we all start out this way. In this state your spiritual nature has not been initialized (It is dead!). You live mostly with your emotions, which interacts with the external physical world. The natural man uses his mind to make decisions and his body to take physical action. He lives in a spiritually dead state. Satan is free to implant thoughts into his mind and has blinded him to spiritual truth (2 Corinthians 4:4). He is separated from Holy God and his mind needs to be renewed.

His self sits on the throne of his being and controls his life based upon his five senses. Once he realizes his need of forgiveness of bad choices (sin), and surrenders his life to Jesus for the forgiveness of his sins, he then becomes what is called an infant or carnal Christian. Christ's spirit (Holy Spirit) enters his spirit and begins making inputs into his mind. He has asserted faith and agreed to the covenant of forgiveness of his sins with God. In the eyes of God, he has been forgiven and saved from the penalty of his sins. He has been justified in God's sight. His position is now with Christ in His kingdom. However, Christ is still hanging on the cross and self is still on the throne of control in his spirit!

The Holy Spirit seals his salvation and nothing will ever take it away from him. He is called a carnal Christian because he retains control of all aspects of his life. As a carnal Christian, he has valuable treasure inside a vessel represented by his body. Unfortunately, for lack of discipleship, he remains carnal, and continues to depend upon his five senses rather than the treasure (Christ represented by the Holy Spirit) inside.

Discipleship or sanctification will transform him into a spiritual man. He has exchanged positions with Christ by giving Christ the throne of his life and crucified his old self-life. He now has a new self with a renewed mind.

What is the Kingdom of God and how do you enter?

If you will examine the Bible closely, you will note that Jesus' emphasis in His teaching was about the nearness of the kingdom of God. You are told to seek first the kingdom of God and His righteousness and all necessary things will be given to you as well (Matthew 6:33). This scripture is not about heaven after you die. It is about the kingdom that is all about you now. Residing in this present kingdom is how to be equipped to change the world.

Obedience Assignment: ☐

4. Pray for the expansion of your kingdom borders by placing your kingdom under His kingdom.

To live strongly and creatively in the kingdom of God, you need to have firmly fixed in your mind what your future is to be like. Your future must make sense to you. It must be something you can now plan or make decisions in terms of, with clarity and joyful anticipation. In this way, your future will be incorporated into your life now. In order to implement something like this process, you must make sure that Christlikeness is in fact the substance of your life. You must truly love the Lord with all your heart, soul, mind, and strength, or you will never be successful in training others to do so.

Your kingdom is simply the range of your effective will. Whatever you genuinely have dominion over is in your kingdom. God's kingdom or rule is the range of His effective will, where what he wants is done. When you submit what and where you are to God, your rule or dominion then increases. True Christian kingdom life is placing your kingdom in His kingdom.

Jesus' own gospel of the kingdom was not that the kingdom was about to come, or had recently come into existence. Jesus' good news was that the kingdom of God had come, and that He, Jesus, was the way or doorway into that kingdom for all men.

If we believe what He actually said, it becomes clear that His gospel concerned the new accessibility of the kingdom to humanity through Himself now.

Where to Begin:

The process must start with your personal transformation. With understanding of how you function and God's plan for the advancement of His kingdom, you will need to practice daily disciplines that establish and sustain your relationship with Jesus. He invites you to join Him by wearing His yoke so that you become a co-conspirator with Him rather than you trying to accomplish great works for Him alone. Jesus clearly declares that you cannot accomplish anything (spiritually) apart from Him (John 15:5). Conversely, the Bible assures you that you can do all things through Christ who strengthens you (Philippians 4:13).

The obedience assignments located throughout this book will facilitate your close, daily fellowship with Jesus if you will faithfully practice them. Obedience is what is missing from churches and individual Christians and therein is our problem. God prefers obedience to works (1 Samuel 15:32). We are often distracted by good social works that consume us and leave us with an attitude of not having time for obedience to His commandments and commissions!

The Invitation

You have received an invitation. You are invited to make a pilgrimage into the heart and life of God. The invitation has long been on public record. You can hardly look anywhere across the human scene and not encounter it. It is literally "blowing in the wind". A door of welcome is open to everyone without exception. No person or circumstance other than his or her own decision can keep anyone away. Whosoever will may come.

The major problem with the invitation now is over-familiarity. Familiarity breeds unfamiliarity — unsuspected unfamiliarity. It looks like other graffiti and even shows up in the same places. Your invitation is to become part of the divine conspiracy to change the world.

God's desire for you is that you should live in Him. He sends among us the Way to Himself. That shows what, in His heart of hearts, God is really like, what reality is really like. God makes Himself and His kingdom available, not in every way human beings have imagined, but in a simple way. The Way we speak of is Jesus, the luminous Nazarene, as Albert Einstein once called Him. Along with two thieves, the authorities executed Him about two thousand years ago. Yet, today, from countless paintings, statues and buildings, from literature and history, from profanity, popular song, and entertainment media, from legend and ritual — Jesus stands quietly at the center of the contemporary world. He so graced the ugly instrument on which he died that the cross has become the most widely exhibited and recognized symbol on earth.

Obedience Assignment: ☐

> 5. Believe that you have entered His courts with thanksgiving.

Think of visiting in a home where you have not been before, it is a large house, and you sit for a while with your host in a living room or on the veranda. Dinner is announced, and he ushers you down a hall, saying at a certain point, "Turn, for the dining room is at hand", or more likely, here is the dining room. Jesus invites you to step into His kingdom with the same clear directions. Where God's will is being accomplished, the kingdom of God is right beside us. It is indeed the kingdom among us.

Be a Co-Conspirator with Jesus

Christ invites you to take part in His kingdom now, as partners with God in a divine conspiracy. A conspiracy is an organized and deliberate plan by two or more to change a situation. The divine conspiracy referred to in this book is you and Jesus organizing and deliberately planning to change the world. Evil and sin abound but it need not be this way. Christians are called to apprentice to Jesus, to patiently but methodically conspire to change the current evil to good.

Obedience Assignment: ☐

6. Silently ask Jesus to commission you as one of His disciples and use you as a co-conspirator with Him.

If you are not truly a disciple, you are missing the opportunity to join the divine conspiracy, the collaboration with God here and now, where He is at work renewing His creation. He invites you into partnership. The person of God Himself and the action of His will are the organizing principles of His kingdom. Everything that obeys those principles, whether by nature or by choice, is within His kingdom.

This exhilarating role as co-conspirator with Jesus is the purpose for which you were born. Simply showing up to church-related things is not discipleship. Not by a long shot. You were created to participate in the kingdom among us as well as the kingdom of heaven after you die, and that participation should be evidence of Jesus' life within you (sort of like light coming into darkness).

The human job description found in chapter one of Genesis indicates that God assigned to you the rule over all living things on earth; animal, and plant. You are responsible before God for life on the earth. However unlikely it may seem from your current viewpoint, God equipped you for this task by forming your nature to function in a conscious, personal relationship of interactive responsibility with Him. You are meant to exercise your rule only in union with Jesus, as He acts with you. He intends to be your constant companion or co-worker in the creative enterprise of life on earth. He wants you to share His yoke, which will result in rest and kingdom fruitfulness. That is what His love for you means in practical terms.

Obedience Assignment: ☐

> 7. Ask Jesus to remind you that you are in His Kingdom.

Jesus offers Himself as the doorway into the life that is truly life. Confidence in Him leads you today, as in other times, to become His apprentice in eternal living.

However, intelligent, effectual entry into this life is obstructed by clouds of well-intentioned misinformation. The gospels that predominate where He is most frequently invoked speak mostly of preparing to die or else of correcting current social practices and conditions. Both are matters of great importance, but neither taps the depths of the reality of Christ's gospel. The usual gospels are, in their effects, nothing less than a standing invitation to omit Jesus from the course of our daily existence! Good can be the enemy of the best. Social ministries must never be substituted for discipleship in Christ. Be very careful to not get distracted by good things to do and allow such good things to crowd out the best — residing in His kingdom now.

Do Not Get Distracted

It is so easy to get distracted. Many good things are being pursued by Christians that are time consuming and interfere with your focus on the primary objectives. For example, Bible study, church planting, mission trips, and Christian music are good but not what Jesus commissioned.

He commissioned you to depend upon Him, go, disciple the nations, baptize them in the name of the Father, Son, and Holy Spirit, and teach them to obey all that He has taught you.

His commission will result in a sustained world-changing movement whereas these other "good" things will not. Substituting faithful church meeting attendance and other outward religious routines and seeking special status of ecstatic experiences is not following the commission He gave us.

Obedience Assignment: ☐

> 8. Think about how you spend your days. Are you cooperating and communing with Jesus? Commit to re-prioritizing your time.

Jesus told the Apostle Peter that He would build His church on the foundation of God's inspired word. Jesus commissioned His apprentices to make disciples that will make disciples. The Apostle Paul repeated this to his disciple Timothy in 2 Timothy 2:2. Too often, we reverse His instructions by trying to build our church and fail to make disciples.

Obedience is access to the abundant life available now. Kingdom obedience is kingdom abundance. They are not two separate things. The inner condition of your soul from which your strength, love, and peace flow (abundance) is the very same condition that generously blesses the oppressor and lovingly offers the other cheek (obedience). However, this truth about obedience seems like a very well kept secret today. And the correlation between knowledge of Christ and the obedience/abundance of life in Christ has now become, apparently, something of a mystery. You must move beyond living with knowledge about Christ to living your life in Christ. A mind renewed, the mind of Christ, is necessary.

This curriculum for Christlikeness is designed for you to seriously and expectantly transition into His promised abundance so you can join Him to change the world. You now live in the outcome of a largely unconscious historical drift over many years!

There is a lack of a serious and expectant intention to bring you and Jesus' people into obedience and abundance through training. That is discipleship as He gave it to us.

Obedience Assignment: ☐

> 9. Ponder the depth and significance of the broad road of Matthew 7:13-14. Do you just know about this scripture or do you really believe it? Do you know anyone on the broad road?

As you approach this task, it is very important to understand that the "teaching" to be done is not a matter of collecting or conveying information. Usually, that will have already been done. You possess almost all of the correct information. If tested for accuracy, you would probably pass. The purpose is not to inform you about things that Jesus believed, taught, and practiced. Somehow the seriously thought out intention, not just a vague idea or wish, to actually bring about the fullness of life in Christ must be reestablished.

Renewed Minds

It should be obvious that the emphasis of the modern church is failing the purpose for which Jesus created her. Our religious tenants must be tested against our commission to make disciples that will make disciples and be rejected if they do not. Thus, valuable time and resources must be applied to obedience, which will lead to abundance.

Obedience Assignment: ☐

> 10. Trust Jesus to accompany you to share your faith with a family member, neighbor, or someone in a hospital, rest home, or recovery center. Leave the results with Him.

Individual minds must be renewed by entering into God's kingdom life rather than just keep studying the Bible! The knowledge already stored in your mind must be put into practice so the resulting experiences will be transformational.

You must move from classroom learning sessions to laboratory-like applications to confirm the validity of what you have learned in the classroom. You must also prompt others to follow you. Your Character has been formed by the culture and environment you have been living in (i.e. worldly – of the flesh)! Your inner being (Character) must be transformed by the renewing of your mind.

Not providing such laboratory opportunities is a major failure of the modern church. Christians are being misled when they believe that their Christian life is being fulfilled by attending church meetings rather than expressing their faith as lights in a very dark world. To live like Christ, you must not retreat into bubbles of safe fellowship with like believers. Like Jesus, you must take the gospel to sinners where they are (outside the walls of your church buildings) to grow the kingdom rather than just add church members!

What Are You Trying To Accomplish in Life - What Is Your Purpose?

The two primary objectives of your Curriculum for Christlikeness are 1. Love and constantly delight in God as your divine creator, and 2. Free you of domination or enslavement to your old patterns of thoughts, feelings, and actions.

If you do not know your purpose in life, you will miss the one opportunity you have to lay up treasure in heaven. Hebrews 9:27 informs you that you will die once (physically) then follows judgment. There will be no re-incarnation or second chance to get life right. Every moment should be carefully redeemed in view of eternity.

USA currency has In God We Trust on every bill and coin. You must practice the reality of God rather than just read about Him. He must renew your mind for your eternal future and for the following generations for which you are responsible.

People are clamoring for evidence of God's realness but do not see such evidence from our churches. Yet, God has promised to manifest Himself to you if you will truly seek Him with all of your heart.

Take Time to Smell the Roses

What does it mean to take time to smell the roses? To enjoy the rose, it is necessary for you to focus on the rose and bring the rose as fully before your senses and mind as possible. To smell a rose, you must get close, and you must linger. Remember who created roses.

When you do so, you delight in it. You Love it. You are to love God like that and have your life filled with His love. God in His glorious reality must be brought before your mind and kept there in such a way that your mind takes root and stays fixed there.

Obedience Assignment: ☐

> 11. Take time to examine the beauty of a rose. Do you really believe a rose just evolved by random chance over a long period of time?

What simply occupies your mind very largely governs what you do. It sets the emotional tone out of which your actions flow.

So much evidence of the reality of our Creator God surrounds you. Just examining the flowers in our back yard and the stars over our roof alone convinces us of His presence.

His colorful migratory birds that pass through that same yard annually competing with the squirrels for birdseed in our feeder provide continuous entertainment and amusement.

So much evidence of the reality of your Creator God surrounds you. With renewed minds, you will see the beauty and variety of life and objects all around you as having been created by Him.

Consumer Christianity is now Normative!

The consumer Christian is one who utilizes the grace of God for forgiveness and the services of the church for special occasions, but does not give his or her life and innermost thoughts, feelings, and intentions over to the kingdom of God. Such Christians are not inwardly transformed and not committed to transformation. Because of this, they remain not just imperfect, for all of us remain imperfect, but routinely and seriously unable and unwilling to do the good they know they can do. Their lives are dominated by fear, greed, impatience, egotism, bodily desires, and the like, and they continue to make provision for them.

Unfortunately, many churches are responding to the consumer appetite of the world rather than focusing on the first commandment. Too many Christians are seeking safety, fun, entertainment, comfort, friends of like thinking, etc. rather than seeking God with their whole hearts. Consequently, churches are dying for lack of God's manifest blessings.

If we can enjoy His presence in our backyard and the solitude of our secret place, why is He not enjoyed by multitudes of people in our little town with approximately 25 churches?

The American dream mindset of selfish gratification has drifted into the modern church. People actually shop for churches that they think will fulfill their personal needs rather than a church where they will be equipped and encouraged to practice Christian discipleship.

Obedience Assignment: ☐

It is unfortunate that many churches appeal to this consumer mindset by offering games, free pizza, baby-sitting, and entertainment in an effort to attract community people to attend their meetings and help finance their organization rather than making disciples to change the world.

> 12. Make an honest assessment of your reason for attending church services. Are you attending to gain anything or to be equipped to serve?

Christian leaders, in their appeal to consumers, often spend more financial and manpower resources on making the church grounds and building attractive and comfortable than for the eternal destinies of those attending the church!

Jesus, in stating that loving the Lord your God with all your heart, soul, mind and strength as the primary, or first commandment, understood that if such love were in place all else of importance would follow, including hearing and doing. The content of the Gospel must become a permanent presence and possession of your mind.

The Bible is clear with verses like Romans 3:23 that we have all sinned and fall short of the perfect glory of our wonderful God and the consequences of our sin is eternal spiritual death or eternal separation from Him. You need to study the gospels (good news) in Matthew, Mark, Luke, and John with intent to obey.

You have a serious problem as a result of your sin. You cannot contaminate heaven by taking your sin into that holy place and you cannot rid yourself of sin. You must have a savior. God loves you so much that He has provided the only way to rid yourself of sin and that one way is through faith in His Son Jesus.

Careful study of Jesus' sermon on the mount found in Matthew 5-7 indicates that His kingdom is available to everyone now; poor, meek, humble, etc., not just those that are viewed as being of benefit to the local church.

Remember Me

Renewal of your mind is best facilitated by practicing daily disciplines and remembering what Jesus has done for you. Practicing daily Christian disciplines is necessary so that you can enjoy a quality and free life now, and be assured of spending eternity with Him in heaven after you die. He suffered many hardships and disappointments, rejection, abandonment, false accusations, abuse, torture, and ultimately execution as if He was a common criminal for you. This is how God was treated! While nailed to that painful cross, He also took upon Himself your sins (as well as all the sins of the world)! For the first time in eternity, Holy Father turned from His Son due to your sins. He took those sins to the grave and left them there as He was cleansed by His own blood and resurrected back to life.

Following His resurrection, Jesus instructed His disciples to wait until they were empowered by the Holy Spirit before attempting to share the gospel with others. His work on earth complete, He now sits at the right hand of the Father making daily intercessions for you.

Obedience Assignment: ☐

13. Pause to envision how God in the Person of Jesus was treated while on His mission to save you. Do you remember Him and love Him?

You too, must be spiritually empowered before you can expect to be productive in kingdom work. Jesus shared the parable of the vineyard to clearly illustrate that you can do nothing apart from Him. You must abide or remain attached to Christ (John 15).

First, You must remember His beauty, truth, and power while He lived among us as one human being among others. The content of the Gospels must become a permanent presence and possession of your mind.

Second, You must remember the way He went to execution as a common criminal among other criminals on your behalf. That is the good reason to wear or display a cross. One displaying it is saying, "I am bought by the sufferings and death of Jesus and I belong to God". The Divine conspiracy of which you can be a part stands over human history in the form of the cross.

Obedience Assignment: ☐

> 14. If you do not wear a cross, seriously consider doing so as your public claim to follow Him.

You must have indelibly imprinted upon your soul the reality of this wonderful person who walked among us and suffered a cruel death to enable you to have life everlasting in God. It should become something that is never beyond the margins of your consciousness!

Third, you are to experience Jesus in His ecclesia, His motley but glorious crew of called out ones. Therefore, the continuing incarnation of the divine Son in His gathered people must fill your mind if you are to love Him and His Father adequately and thus live on the Rock of hearing and doing.

Jesus started His church for the purpose of evangelizing and discipling the whole world. His church should be an equipping center for processing converts into mature disciples. He told His disciples that if they would follow Him, He would make them fishers of men. One of our dear friends commented that if a Christian is not fishing for men, he is not following Christ!

People complain about the uncomfortable seats and stale popcorn when center stage is empty of the main event. These elements are nice sideshows, but people do not come to church for the carnival rides. They come to meet God. Despite all the opinions churchless (and churched) people offer about musical styles, architecture, sound systems, creativity, intellectualism, and the menu of programs provided by churches, none of these is the main attraction.

You have plenty of other opportunities to gather with people you do not know for conversation, music, education, and personal enrichment. However, a local body of believers is the only place you can meet God_together with His people.

Fourth, you must acknowledge that Jesus is the master of the created universe and of human history. He is the one in control of all the atoms, particles, and galaxies of the universe. All of the physical cosmos depends upon Him. It is He as the logos, which maintains and manipulates the ultimate laws of the physical universe.

Thoroughly presented in these four ways, the love of Jesus for you, and the magnificence of His person, will bring you to adore Him. His love and loveliness should fill your life. Once you come to know the love of Jesus Christ, nothing else in the world will seem as beautiful or desirable.

Acquiring the Habits of Goodness.

Another area of teaching required to bring you to the place where you love the Lord with all your heart, soul, mind, and strength concerns the goodness of your own existence, the life made through your natural birth and the following course of your life. You will never have the easy, unhesitating love of God that makes obedience to Jesus your natural response unless you are sure that it is good for you to be who you are.

This means you must have no doubt that when, where, and to whom you were born is good, and that nothing irredeemable has happened to you or can happen to you on your way to your destiny in God's full world.

Obedience Assignment: ☐

> 15. Think about how complex you are. The eternal you lives in a temporary body that is marvelously made.

God, as your faithful Creator and as presented in the face of Jesus Christ, is lovely and magnificent. However, He will remain something to be admired and even worshiped at a distance if that is all you know of Him.

In order for you to be brought into a full and joyous love of God, you must see your own life within the framework of unqualified goodness.

It is vital to honor your father and mother. Most of your doubts about the goodness of your life concern very specific matters: your parents and family, your body, your marriage and children (or lack thereof), your opportunities in life, your work and calling, etc. At the heart of your identity lie your family and, specifically, your parents. You cannot be thankful for who you are unless you can be thankful for them.

Obedience Assignment: ☐

> 16. If your parents are living, let them know that you love and appreciate them.

Our families were financially poor but we did not know it. Our parents sacrificed much for our health, education, and maturity. As we reflect on our lives of the past 85 years, we can clearly see God's guidance through our parents and circumstances.

This is part of a process that must go hand in hand with the second main objective in your curriculum for Christlikeness.

That is the breaking of the power of patterns of wrongdoing and evil that govern your life because of your long habitation in a world alienated from God.

Breaking Bondage to the Sin in Your Body

You must learn to recognize these habitual patterns for what they are and escape from their grip. The pattern of wrongdoing that governs your life outside the kingdom are usually quite weak, they are simply your habits, your largely automatic responses to thoughts, and feelings. Typically, you act wrongly before reflecting. This is what gives bad habits their power! For the most part they are, as the Apostle Paul knew, actual characteristics of your body and your social context.

They do not bother to run through your conscious mind or deliberative will. It is rare that what you do wrong is a result of careful deliberation. Your routine behavior manages to keep your conscious mind off balance and on the defensive. You defend what you have done by doing further wrong: denying, misleading, and rationalizing, etc.

You will never be able to deal with that evil as long as you take it to be external to yourself or something other than precisely the humdrum routines you accept as your habits. Nothing has the power to tempt you or move you to wrong action that you have not permitted to be in you!

The most spiritually dangerous things in you are the little habits of thought, feeling, and action that you regard as normal because everyone is like that – it is only human.

Death to self is simply the acceptance of this fact. It is the cross applied to daily existence that you must learn in order to break the grip of the sin in your members that drive you.

The training required to transform your most basic habits of thought, feeling, and action will not be done for you. Yet it is something that you cannot do by yourself. Life in all its forms must reach out to what is beyond it to achieve fulfillment, and so it is with the spiritual life. The familiar words of Jesus are, "I am the vine; you are the branches. If you remain in me and I in you, you will bear much fruit; apart from me you can do nothing." (John 15:5). There must be balance, in general, if you do nothing it will certainly be without Him! Kingdom life is a cooperative life with Jesus.

A triangle is used to illustrate the factors involved in the transformation of your life from inside (the mind) out (behavior). The image is designed to suggest the correlation in practical life that can certainly lead to the transformation of your inner self into Christlikeness.

The intervention of the Holy Spirit is placed at the apex of the triangle to indicate His primacy in the entire process. Jesus said, "I tell you the truth no-one can enter the Kingdom of God unless he is born of water and the Spirit" (John 3:5).

As a Spiritual man, you are not in the realm of the flesh but are in the realm of the Spirit, if indeed, the Spirit of God lives in you. Moreover, if you do not have the Spirit of Christ, you do not belong to Christ. But if Christ is in you, then even though your body is subject to death because of sin, the Spirit gives life because of righteousness (Romans 8:9-10).

The Indispensable Role of Tests

Therefore being justified by faith, you have peace with God through your Lord Jesus Christ (Romans 5:1). This is not only so, but you also rejoice in your sufferings, because you know that suffering produces perseverance; perseverance, character, and character, hope.

The trials of your daily life and your activities specially planned for transformation are placed at the bottom of the triangle to indicate that where the transformation is actually carried out is in your real life, where you dwell with God and your neighbors. At the level of real life, the role of what is imposed upon you (trials) goes hand in hand with your choices as to what you will do with yourself.

"Consider it pure joy, my brothers and sisters,[a] whenever you face trials of many kinds, because you know that the testing of your faith produces perseverance. Let perseverance finish its work so that you may be mature and complete, not lacking anything" (James 1:2-4).

God engineers the daily circumstances of your life. He has a good reason for arranging hardships, tribulations, and tests to build your character.

A Christian's response often results in rebellion rather than patience, which is the desired response.

Obedience Assignment: ☐

> 17. When your next "test" occurs, let it become a character building opportunity. Respond with a positive rather than a negative reaction.

Character building is always accomplished by enduring hardships. Suffering for Jesus' sake is highly valued in the Bible.

Spiritual Disciplines to Renew Your Mind

A discipline is any activity within your power that you engage in to enable you to do what you cannot do by direct effort. Practicing can be a discipline as in shooting baskets, playing a musical instrument, typing, etc. Spiritual disciplines are designed to help you be active and effective in the spiritual realm of your own heart, being spiritually alive by grace in relation to God and His kingdom. They are designed to help you withdraw from total dependence on the merely human or natural and to depend on the ultimate reality, which is God and His kingdom.

A step is something only you can take. The training that leads to doing what you hear from Jesus must therefore involve first, the purposeful disruption of your automatic thoughts, feelings, and actions by doing different things with your body.

Therefore, as God's chosen people, holy and dearly loved, clothe yourselves with compassion, kindness, humility, gentleness and patience. Bear with each other and forgive one another if any of you has a grievance against someone. Forgive as the Lord forgave you. Moreover, over all these virtues put on love, which binds them all together in perfect unity.

Let the peace of Christ rule in your hearts, since as members of one body you were called to peace. And be thankful. Let the message of Christ dwell among you richly as you teach and admonish one another with all wisdom through psalms, hymns, and songs from the Spirit, singing to God with gratitude in your hearts. And whatever you do, whether in word or deed, do it all in the name of the Lord Jesus, giving thanks to God the Father through him. (Colossians 3:12-17).

Obedience Assignment: ☐

18. Use your secret place away from human sounds to practice daily spiritual disciplines. Start a journal of daily thoughts and prayers.

For this very reason, make every effort to add to your faith goodness; and to goodness, knowledge; and to knowledge, self-control; and to self-control, perseverance; and to perseverance, godliness; and to godliness, mutual affection; and to mutual affection, love. For if you possess these qualities in increasing measure, they will keep you from being ineffective and unproductive in your knowledge of our Lord Jesus Christ (2 Peter 1:5-8). If you lack these things, you are blind and shortsighted and have forgotten the cleansing from your past sins. Therefore, make every effort to confirm your calling. If you do, these things will never fail you.

Rather, clothe yourselves with the Lord Jesus Christ, and do not think about how to gratify the desires of the flesh (Romans 13:14).

Model Your Life upon Jesus Himself

A further help in understanding what spiritual disciplines are for you is to recognize them as simply a matter of following Jesus' practices. To put off the old person and put on the new you need to follow Jesus into the activities that He engaged in to nurture His life in relation to the Father. His use of solitude, silence, study of scripture, prayer, and service to others were all disciplinary actions in His life. There is no complete list of spiritual disciplines but a small number of them are central to spiritual growth.

Two important disciplines of abstinence are solitude and silence. Liberation from your own desires is one of the greatest gifts of solitude and silence. Old bondages to wrongdoing will begin to drop off as you see them for what they are. The possibility of really loving people will dawn upon you. You will soon know what it is to live by Grace rather than just talk about it.

Obedience Assignment: ☐

Two important disciplines of positive engagement are study and worship.

John and Dot Overton

Once Solitude has done its work, the key to progression is study. It is in study that you place your mind fully upon God and His kingdom. Study is brought to its natural completion in the worship of God.

> 19. Write your relationship with Jesus in two sentences. This will be your story.

We have briefly touched on four specific spiritual disciplines – solitude and silence and study and worship. It must be clear how strongly you will be nourished by the first principle to love God with heart, soul, mind, and strength. Other disciplines, such as fasting, service to others, fellowship, and so on might be practiced as well but if these four are pursued with intelligence and prayer, whatever else is needed will certainly come along.

Sanctification (Discipleship) Must Follow Justification

Obedience Assignment: ☐

> 20. Take one step of obedience. Be careful to not back down the steps - keep moving forward.

You should expect change (growth) in which you progress from one stage of your spiritual life in God to another.

Numerous programs in local congregations and wider levels of organizations are frequently spoken of as discipleship. Everything from Sunday school, special courses and seminars to twelve-step programs.

Obedience Assignment: ☐

> 21. Write how you will relate your story to the Gospel. This will be Your Bridge to the Gospel. Be brief.

They do not, however, reach the root of the human problem.

That root is the character of the inner life, where Jesus and His call to apprenticeship in the kingdom place emphasis.

We are all physically born into a kingdom of darkness the Bible refers to as the world (natural man). Due to sin, this kingdom has come under the governance of our spiritual enemy, Satan. He influences you to think that self is in control. If you fail to recognize your sinful nature in this domain, and reject God's grace offer of forgiveness, your eternal destiny will be the grave, hell, and ultimately the lake of fire totally separated from God.

Alternatively, if you follow Jesus by taking up your cross daily and becoming one of His disciples, you will transition into the kingdom of God under the governance of Jesus now which ultimately leads to eternal paradise, and heaven with God. I have been crucified with Christ and I no longer live, but Christ lives in me. The life I now live in the body, I live by faith in the Son of God, who loved me and gave himself for me (Spiritual man - Galatians 2:20).

We were therefore buried with him through baptism into death in order that, just as Christ was raised from the dead through the glory of the Father, we too may live a new life. For if we have been united with him in a death like his, we will certainly also be united with him in a resurrection like his (Romans 6:4-5). For the wages of sin is death, but the gift of God is eternal life in Christ Jesus our Lord (Romans 6:23).

Living in the eternal kingdom of God starts now for the Christian. For he has rescued us from the dominion of darkness and brought us into the kingdom of the Son he loves (Colossians 1: 13).

Therefore, if anyone is in Christ, the new creation has come. The old has gone, the new is here (2 Corinthians 5:17).

Your mind will be renewed if you allow the right things to be added, The written Word/ the Bible. If you add water, even a small amount, to the fuel tank of your car, it will not perform as it was designed. Only if you purge the tank and refill with the proper fuel will your car operate properly. You must approach your walk with Christ in a similar way. You are not designed to run on just anything you may fill your mind with.

Obedience Assignment: ☐

> 22. Write John 3:16.
> Use this verse as the
> Gospel - (Good News).

Perhaps you have never been told what to do. You have been misinformed about your part in eternal living. On the other hand, maybe you have heard something that is right-on with Jesus Himself, but misunderstood it. But grow in the grace and knowledge of our Lord and Savior Jesus Christ. To him be glory both now and forever (2 Peter 3:18). However, there is the problem! Even a Christian that is not regularly nurtured by consumption of the written word and prompted by the Holy Spirit will live wilted, unfruitful lives.

Great Omissions from the Great Commission

There is an obvious great disparity between, the hope for life expressed in Jesus — found in the Bible and in many examples from His followers. On the other hand, the actual day-to-day behavior, inner life, and social presence of most of those who now profess adherence to Him often seem no different from those living apart from Christ.

The New Testament literature, which must define your terms if you are ever to get your bearings in the Way with Christ, makes this clear. In that context, you are a person who does not just profess certain views as your own but applies your growing understanding of life in the kingdom of God to every aspect of your life on earth. In contrast, the governing assumption today, among professing Christians, is that you can be Christian forever and never become a disciple! What Jesus expects you to do is not complicated or obscure. In some cases, it will require that you change what you have been doing. The great commission provides His plan for spiritual formation, church growth, and the desire to change the world. Let's just do it.

Obedience Assignment: ☐

> 23. Write out a list of people you know that are away from God.

The word disciple occurs 269 times in the New Testament. Christian is found three times and was first introduced to refer primarily to disciples of Jesus (Acts 11:26). The New Testament is a book about disciples, by disciples, and for disciples of Jesus Christ.

In place of Christ's plan, historical drift has been substituted! Make converts (to a particular faith and practice) and baptize them into church membership. This causes two great omissions from the great commission to stand out: the making of disciples, and enrolling people as Christ's students, when we should let all else wait for that. Then we also omit the step of taking our converts through training that will bring them closer to what Jesus directed.

Most Christians are far more concerned about growing or restoring their church than changing the world. Yet, we have a clear commission to be visionary on a global scale. Jesus told Peter that He would take care of His church and the gates of hell shall not prevail against it (Matthew 16:18).

It is very important to understand that the "teaching" to be done at this point is not a matter of just collecting or conveying information! Special experiences, faithfulness to the church, correct doctrine, and external conformity to the teachings of Jesus all come along as appropriate, more or less automatically.

Failure due to Lack of Proper Foundations

Obedience Assignment: □

> 24. Study the Gospels; Matthew, Mark, Luke and John. Add a list of Jesus' commandments, commissions, and instructions in your journal.

Your Life will be a failure if not built on proper foundations. You must perform foundation building daily, else you will become adrift!

Jesus said, "If you love me, keep my commandments" (John 14:15). Keeping the commands of Jesus begins with recognizing what they are. Let His words renew your mind.

Now that you have completed your Curriculum for Christlikeness and practiced the Obedience Assignments identified therein, continue with your plan to change the world by studying Phase II, Equipping Parents. Select up to three couples to assist you by teaching them Phase II of this process.

Obedience Assignment: ☐

25. Take a few moments to check out our website at www.equippingstudents.com.

Apply to become an Equipping Students (ES) manager. Husband / wife teams are preferred as ES managers since some of the future instructions should be taught by a woman and some by a man.

Phase II

Equipping Parents (EP):

Equipping Parents (EP) is the second phase of the change the world process. EP should be taught by an ES Manager that has completed the curriculum for Christlikeness. EP is designed to equip parents to

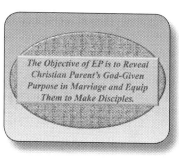

The Objective of EP is to Reveal Christian Parent's God-Given Purpose in Marriage and Equip Them to Make Disciples.

live the gospel of Christ in their homes and communities, and start a sustained, global, Christian movement.

Obedience Assignment: ☐

> 26. While in your secret place, honestly write what your purpose is in life. If you are not sure, say so.

EP raises the bar of expectation for parents and holds them accountable for their children's discipleship. Phase III, Equipping Students (ES), is our ultimate goal for starting sustained Christian movements on school campuses but EP training should precede ES to identify qualified Christian helpers to apply ES to students.

The first of eight parent discipleship sessions is titled

Know Your Purpose. This most important session is designed to make sure the parents being discipled are Christians with sound Biblical foundations for growing in Christ. They will be helped to know their life purpose or be are willing to embark on a path to reveal their purpose.

Our Current Context:

The secular culture is radically changing for the worse and luring people of all age groups away from the church and many away from Christianity. EP is designed to reverse this trend and start building family lives on solid Christian foundations. Absence of influence by Christian nuclear families (husband, wife, children), and healthy churches is resulting in whole communities becoming vulnerable to Satanic attacks. Moral and ethical standards are adrift for lack of sound Judeo-Christian foundations.

Data from the Barna Group illustrates the urgency of the current situation (www.barna.org/research). Barna Group is a visionary research and resource company located in Ventura, California.

Obedience Assignment: ☐

27. Take a few moments to check out the Barna Group. www.barna.org/research

Started in 1984, the firm is widely considered a leading research organization focused on the intersection of faith and culture. In their 30 + year history, Barna Group has conducted more than one million interviews over the course of hundreds of studies, and has become a go-to source for insights about faith and culture, leadership and vocation, and generations. Barna Group has tracked the role of faith in America, developing one of the nation's most comprehensive databases of spiritual indicators.

Barna Group research shows that 28% of Elders (over age 70) are post Christians. This is the resource age God has placed in our churches. Being retired, they have time, experience, education, and wealth. 35% of Boomers (ages 51 to 69) are post Christians. They have raised their children and should be prepared to take the mantle of Christian leadership. 40% of Busters (ages 30 to 50) are post Christians. They are the most influential on the next generation, and 48% of Mosaics / Millennials (ages 13 to 29) are post Christians. They are the future of Christianity!

Why Equip Parents:

Barna research reveals that during the 1960s, polls showed the three most influential factors in a child's life to be 1) Parents, 2) Teachers, and 3) Spiritual Leaders. Today, the three most influential factors in a child's life are 1) Friends, 2) Media, and 3) Parents. Spiritual leaders dropped to 17th! Friends often have more influence on married couples, their children, and students than personal convictions, parents, or God!

Thus, the reasons the target EP group is parents are 1) they are the second largest group leaving the church. 2) They are responsible for the next generation. 3) They instill the earliest and most lasting influence in their children's character and discipline. 4) They are relational, energetic, available, and influential with other couples. And 5) they will prepare their children for marriage, and the introduction of the following generations to Christianity.

Where to Begin: The Biblical process for building lives on proper foundations starts with the nuclear family: father, mother, and children (Ephesians 6:1-4). The interrelationships practiced in the family sets the future of the next generation. Young children's observation of their parent's lifestyle has more influence on them than any other factor and when they are old, they will not depart from it. Please do more than just drop them off at Sunday school. You must be their spiritual example and teach them as their parents.

A modern day tragedy is a parent's failure to raise their children in the love and admonition of the Lord so that when they grow up, they will not depart from Him (Proverbs 6:22). Rather, they look for ways to delegate their responsibility to churches, schools, day care, etc. so they will be free to pursue their selfish interests!

Obedience Assignment: ☐

28. Honestly assess your church. Is she producing Disciples of Christ? (Y), (N).

Unfortunately, the world system has influenced too many parents to think that they need to give their children presents more than their presence. You can change the world if you will return to the Biblical model of home life. You must start with the current generation.

This self-teaching course is designed to help Christian parents prepare their pre-school, intermediate school, high school, and college students to enjoy free, quality lives and change the world by building their lives on the foundation of Jesus' teachings.

Jesus commissioned all Christians to: Go forth, evangelize, make disciples of the nations, baptize them, teach the new disciples to obey all that He has taught, and perform this commission with the energy and inspiration of the Holy Spirit (Matthew 28:18-20). This commission is designed to start sustained Christian movements across all borders, ethnicities, languages, and social groups. In other words, converts to Christianity are to be equipped to continue the process of converting and discipling others.

Contemporary Christianity often stops with evangelism, and some only for the purpose of gaining church members to support the institution. There are no sustaining results from such emphasis. Many Christian churches are sick and dying for lack of sustaining movement! Secular influence on the church has been slow but relentless. Recovery from this decline will require time to return to the spiritual foundations upon which Christ built His church.

Our schools are the largest concentrated unreached people groups in our neighborhoods. Dysfunctional homes have produced children totally unprepared for the cultural influence being experienced in their schools. Homes are supposed to prepare students for life - eternal life! We hope that you can see and respond to the urgency of identifying Christians (through EP) to apply ES (Phase III) in your local schools.

Children must have a firm Christian foundation built upon Jesus before they enter school. If not, they will be in danger of being influenced to forsake Christ, and be ineffective in influencing others to enter God's kingdom.

Obedience Assignment: ☐

> 29. If you have children, are you raising them to commune with Jesus daily? (Y), (N).

Strong Christian parents must be equipped to raise their children as Disciples of Christ and join Jesus to add other parent couples to the Kingdom of God.

How Sustained EP Networks Work:

EP is a discipleship ministry based upon the great commission (Matthew 28:18-20) targeted to a few married couples. The success of EP depends upon the faithful discipline of Christian manager/teachers in regional communities. The steps to initiate a local EP movement are:

Step 1. - Adult ES managers that have completed Phase I, Curriculum for Christlikeness, must be identified and commissioned to oversee the EP process in their region (You may become a regional ES manager. Contact Equipping Central at www.equippingstudents.com).

Step 2. - ES managers should seek additional adult helpers (teachers/coordinators) to assist in sustaining the movement locally. Helpers may result from couples that complete this EP process.

Step 3. - The ES managers and their adult teacher/coordinators will select a small group of 2 to 3 married couples for discipleship. These parent couples need not be from the same church, denomination, or community. If more than three couples are willing candidates for EP and adult teacher/coordinators are prepared to disciple them, additional EP groups should be started but extra couples must not be added in excess of three.

Step 4. - Following commissioning, the ES managers/ coordinators will teach an eight-week discipleship course to the initial small group of parent couples. The materials for this course are included in a parent binder and on the thumb drive, and may be downloaded from the website.

Step 5. - Near the completion of their eight-week discipleship course, the group of discipled parents will recommend a second group of 2 to 3 parent couples with which they have shared their story.

Step 6. - The adult teacher/coordinators selected in step 2 will equip additional groups of parents using the same eight discipleship lessons.

EP will become a sustaining discipleship movement as the managers continue to recruit adult teacher/ coordinators that will disciple small groups of parents as prescribed in 2 Timothy 2:2 and as each parent group recommends additional parents from their church and communities for EP discipleship.

Obedience Assignment: ☐

> 30. Ask Jesus if He is calling you to become commissioned as an ES manager.

Three Day EP Training: EP training can be self-taught or by an ES manager/teacher. Training materials may be downloaded from the equippingstudents.com website.

Evening of Day One EP Training: The evening training on the first day will be a brief overview of EP. ES managers will oversee EP in their area and report regional results to Equipping Central (EC) by way of the Internet. Those being discipled by EP will train their children and disciple a group of 2 to 3 parent couples by teaching eight one to one and a half hour discipleship sessions in the future. Additional adult Christians may serve as observers during the initial EP cycle in preparation to teach additional small groups of parents.

It is critical that the managers /teachers /coordinators first complete the curriculum for Christlikeness, and be established, born-again Christians that practice daily disciplines of prayer, Bible study, journaling, sharing their faith, etc. They understand and choose to practice the great commandment and great commission. They must be willing to share their experiences as practicing Christians with other couples. Other couples will not likely be responsive to teachers that do not practice what they teach.

The managers need not perform all of the arrangements for the EP course but will seek help from other Christian adults to make sure that all arrangements are made in advance of the initial EP couple instruction.

Obedience Assignment: ☐

> 31. Offer to make your home available for EP discipleship training.

The managers will be responsible for a suitable location to perform the parent training. This facility should have enough space for a class of 2 to 3 parent couples along with several adult observers. The facility should have: 1) Electrical power and an extension cord with at least two outlets, 2) Tables for students to write on, 3) Individual chairs, 4) A screen, or suitable wall for projecting training slides, 5) Restrooms, and 6) Good lighting. Access to a quality copy machine will be very useful. A home, public building, or church may provide a suitable facility for EP training.

The following materials must be secured for each couple before starting a discipleship class: 1) a study Bible, 2), a parent binder containing parent manuals, list of scriptures, EP forms, a journal, children's books, and 4) a quality writing pen. These materials may be downloaded free from the equipping students website or bound copies may be purchased from the website (Special Note: If the parents prefer using their smart phones or tablets for their daily times with the Lord, then the Bibles and journals will not be needed. The estimated cost of these materials in bound form are listed on the website.

The managers will schedule and conduct eight EP classes for the initial group of parents. The adult teacher/coordinators will sit in these classes as monitors in preparation to equip another group of parents in the future.

The first class will be to establish transparent communication between the teachers and the couples.

Obedience Assignment: ☐

32. Write the purpose and scope of EP in your journal.

The managers will explain the purpose and scope of EP and ask for commitment to complete eight approximately one to one and a half hour classes as well as be accountable for accomplishing weekly goals to be set by the class. Each couple must understand what is involved and agree to complete the course or be lovingly removed. The inclination to recruit a large group of parents must be resisted. By restricting the focus to a few selected couples, a multiplying movement is much more likely to be started and sustained. Replacing any dropouts with additional couples must be resisted.

The managers will share their relationship with Jesus and ask each student to tell about their relationship with Jesus. It is crucial that clear verbalization about personal relationships be expressed. This may be awkward for some initially but will become comfortable with experience.

Obedience Assignment: ☐

> 33. Be prepared to share your relationship with Jesus — your story.

During the first class, each couple will use form ES1 in their binder to write their story. Their story (their relationship with Jesus) must be brief and understandable by other parent couples. They are then to write a bridge to the gospel and recite John 3:16. The parents selected for the group should be able to recite John 3:16 but the teachers must be prepared to help them memorize it if they are not. The parents should then use form ES2 to list the names of parents they know that are away from God. Finally, they must select a secret place where they will meet with Jesus daily.

Each couple should be willing to lead the class in prayer. This may also prove awkward at first but is an important part of their training.

A scripture-based vision will be cast and a brief discipleship lesson will be taught by the teacher during each EP session. A set of goals to be accomplished by the parents before the next meeting will be agreed upon. The couples must understand that they will be accountable for reporting the results of their goals at the following meeting.

Near the completion of the first course, the couples will recommend a second group of two to three couples for EP discipleship. The coordinators that monitored the first series of classes will teach the second small group. A different training location may be needed and supplies secured before starting additional classes.

A network of parent coordinators will be recruited to monitor subsequent discipleship classes and each class will recommend additional small groups of parents to be equipped. Thus, EP will become a sustained movement of Christian discipleship among parents. These couples will influence their peers to become followers of Christ.

Training, Basic EP Strategy, Day Two:

The second day will be full of instructions on the EP process, and a brief overview of eight parent-equipping classes. A mid-day break for lunch will be necessary.

Following opening prayer, remind the parent couples of the purpose of EP.

We must have a radical paradigm shift back to Christian basics as outlined in the book of Acts. Our commission is to build the kingdom: start locally (our homes) and move out to the uttermost parts of the world.

EP is for parents that will be a part of a disciplship revolution. EP will only work if both the managers/ teacher/coordinators and the small group of parents commit themselves to faithfully obey New Testament commandments and commissions. They must be absolutely dependent upon the Holy Spirit to accomplish the objectives of EP.

The initial discipleship sessions will be to equip each couple with a Christian foundation. EP will then move the parents from the classroom environment to share their faith with other parents in their community. It is essential that the adult teachers lovingly share their Christian experiences with the parent couples.

Each EP equipping session will include six parts facilitated by an ES teacher and assisted by a parent for some of the parts. Each training session is packed with materials, so great care must be given to keeping the sessions on schedule. An important part of the training is to teach the parents to be brief and communicate clearly so they will be asked to assist with some of the parts of each meeting. Do not call upon the same parent each time but rotate through all of them so they will gain the experience.

Obedience Assignment: ☐

> 34. Be prepared to open the EP session with prayer.

1. Opening Prayer: The teacher should start the first session with prayer for the parents, home, and children. Another should be appointed to be prepared to lead in prayer for the subsequent session.

2. How Are You Doing Spiritually?: During the first session, the teacher should briefly share his/her relationship with Jesus. Emphasize how brief you told your story and inform them that they will be asked to briefly share their relationship with Jesus with the group during future sessions.

3. Loving Acountability: The teacher should explain that the group will agree on goals to be accomplished during the following week and that each parent will be accountable for sharing the results of how their goals were accomplished during the next EP session.

4. Vision Casting: The teacher will cast a Biblical vision for the group each week. Vision casting materials designed to insure a "can-do" attitude are included for each session on the thumb drive and website.

5. Brief Discipleship Lesson: The teacher will teach a brief discipleship lesson for the group each week. Discipleship lessons are also included on the thumb drive and website.

6. Goal Setting: The group will be given goals to accomplish during the following week. They will also be informed that they will each be accountable for sharing how they accomplished their goals at the next equipping session.

Overview of the Eight Parent Discipleship Sessions:

Included on the thumb drive are powerpoint outlines to be used by the teacher and manuals to be used by couples to follow along with the powerpoint images. Vision castings are designed to assure each couple that they can accomplish the goals of EP based upon a Bible scripture and each parent will memorize the scripture as part of their week's goal.

Following are brief outlines for the eight sessions to be facilitated by an ES teacher with assistance from selected parents for some parts of the sessions: (Note: Illustrated Children books are also available for teaching the same eight topics by the parents to their children).

Session Number 1: Know Your Life Purpose is to establish the framework for all future discipleship sessions.

Obedience Assignment: ☐

> 35. Confidently share your purpose in Life.

It is essential that teacher/student transparency be established during the initial session and maintained for the rest of the EP discipleship process. The first session is to make sure the parents being discipled are not just religious but are true Christians. We will camp here until the group has demonstrated that their faith in Christ is indeed authentic. They will memorize Proverbs 3:5-6, and make frequent reference to it throughout their discipleship training, "Trust in the Lord with all your heart and lean not on your own understanding; in all your ways submit to him and he will make your paths straight."

Session Number 2: - Spiritual Disciplines: We must never lose sight of our EP objective, which is to reveal Christian Parent's God-given purpose in marriage and equip them to make Disciples of Christ.

They should bring their, EP binder and pen to all of the following sessions. Starting with the second EP session, parents will be appointed to serve as teacher assistants.

Obedience Assignment: ☐

> 36. Confidently share your daily disciplines.

The EP teacher will serve as the session teacher as well as encourage and coach the parent assistant. Different parent assistants should be appointed for each future EP session. They will memorize Acts 1:8, "But you will receive power when the Holy Spirit comes on you; and you will be my witnesses in Jerusalem, and in all Judea and Samaria, and to the ends of the earth". Parents will be instructed to locate a secret place and start practicing daily spiritual disciplines.

Obedience Assignment: ☐

> 37. Share how you practice staying within moral boundaries.

Session Numbers 3 & 4: - Moral Boundaries: These two sessions will emphasize personal morality character traits. The disciplines being practiced from the previous sessions will be beneficial in drawing moral lines beyond which adult parents will not venture. Avoiding unfaithfullness will be covered in session 3 and self control will be covered in session 4. Always remind the parents that they will be accountable for sharing the results of their goals at the next session. Memorize Philippians 4:13 for session 3, "I can do all this through Him who gives me strength.", and for session 4 Luke 9:23. "Whoever wants to be My disciple must deny themselves and take up their cross daily and follow Me."

Obedience Assignment: ☐

> 38. Be prepared to share how you select and keep friends.

Session Number 5 - Healthy Friendships: The direction parents take in life will be highly influenced by the friends they keep. For the Christian this is a balancing act between influencing others for Christ and being influenced by others for evil. Much care must be given by parents to the friends that they and their children associate with. Memorize Matthew 4:19, "Come, follow me", Jesus said, "and I will send you out to fish for people".

Obedience Assignment: ☐

39. Share how ES is the means for fulfilling your vision.

Session Number 6: - Wise Choices: We all must make choices and our choices have consequences that chart the course of our future, especially our eternal future! Others have made choices that we might consider to be un-wise but many of their choices have led to our benefit: We Are Free! Think of the choices Jesus made. Memorize Proverbs 29:18, "Where there is no revelation (vision) people cast off restraint; but blessed is the one who heeds wisdom's instruction".

Session Number 7: - Ultimate Authority: Our best freedom comes from our obedience to authority: Parents, teachers, law enforcement, spiritual leaders, God. Memorize Matthew 28:18. "All authority in heaven and earth has been given to Me".

Obedience Assignment: ☐

40. Tell the group how you actually prefer others over self.

Session Number 8: - Others First: During the final EP class the group will practice preferring others over self, be recognized as Disciples of

Christ that raise their children in the way they should go, and become fishers of men (other parents).

Obedience Assignment: ☐

41. Share examples of how you submit to those with authority over you.

Memorize Romans 5:8, "But God demonstrates his own love for us in this: While we were still sinners, Christ died for us".

Training, Day Three, Field Training:

Today, the managers /trainers will be taken through an EP laboratory where they will use the tools they have learned to make sure they relate to what their group of parents will be asked to do.

Day 3 will start with breakfast in one of the teacher's homes or a restaurant where privacy can be enjoyed.

Obedience Assignment: ☐

42. Be prepared to share your story, bridge, and the gospel first.

During the course of their time together, they will write their story, prepare a bridge to the Gospel, Memorize John 3:16 and prepare a list of parents that they know are away from God, which may be Christians or non-Christians.

The adults will share their story with each other, and recite John 3:16 like their future students will be expected to do.

After breakfast, the adults will contact one of the parents on their list and invite them to coffee (or tea). The time together should be a pleasant one and unrushed. This should be a loving encounter with no pretense of trying to sell anything or talk them into anything.

During the conversations, tell your story as led by the Holy Spirit. Remember that this must be very brief and easy to understand (i.e. since I have Jesus in my life I have come into a relationship with Him: He has changed me, and given me purpose and eternal life.)

Continue with your bridge to the Gospel (i.e. I am free from my past! You can be too! Can I tell you how?)

Recite John 3:16 as the Gospel (i.e., For God so loved the world that he gave His one and only Son, that whoever believes in him shall not perish but have eternal life).

Ask if you can be of help to your friend. Agree to follow up with them at their convenience. Thank them for responding to your request to enjoy a cup of coffee and assure them that you will be praying for them. Give them a Christian tract and ask if they need a Bible. Copies of an appropriate tract is available from our website and in the parent binder.

Application of the EP tools must be experienced to effectively teach others to use them.

EP Training, Evening of Day Three:

Asking parents to become disciples/equippers raises the bar of expectation radically. In a few years, the children of these parents will be making final preparation for their future. They will marry and become another generation of parents. They will influence our culture economically, morally, and spiritually.

The managers/teachers will meet during the evening to discuss EP, share questions they have and problems they foresee. A time will be used to pray for parents, their children, and their community. Pray that EP will be anointed to start a sustained spiritual awakening among parents.

A Commissioning Service will be conducted during which those that complete the course will be recognized and commissioned with dated EP Certificates.

Obedience Assignment: ☐

43. Be prepared to pray over those that complete the EP training.

Those that agree to start a small group of parents will be provided with EP training kits and shown how to download additional materials from the website.

Obedience Assignment: ☐

44. Be prepared to present them with an EP Certificate of Completion.

Provide EP training kits to those that agree to launch an EP course for other parents (no more than three couples).

Obedience Assignment: ☐

45. Provide training kits to those that agree to teach EP to other parents

Congratulations, you have now completed two of the three phases of this process to change the world.

Obedience Assignment: ☐

> 46. Offer to help organize another EP series or ES series for those certified to teach.

Now for the most important phase that will start a sustained Discipleship movement.

Obedience Assignment: ☐

> 47. Use your secret place to ask Jesus to share His yoke by organizing an ES course in your community.

Phase III targets students to become Disciples of Christ that will take the Gospel onto their campuses.

Many students are from dysfunctional families and therefore ill equipped to cope with evil and temptations that are present on their campuses.

Phase III

Equipping Students (ES):

ES is the ultimate goal of this overall process. Ideally, an ES manager team will have been commissioned for a city, state, or region having completed phases I and II before attempting this primary phase.

Unlike traditional youth ministries, ES raises the bar by equipping students to become Christ's apprentice, share their story, and take the Gospel onto their campuses. Entertainment, food, and games are purposely avoided in ES. Students certified in ES are taught to share their stories with their siblings, peers, parents, and teachers.

The Objective of ES is to Reveal Christian Student's God-Given Purpose in Life So They Will take the Gospel Onto Their Campuses.

Why Equip Students:

The reasons the primary target group for changing the world is students are 1) they represent the future of Christianity and the church, 2) they are the largest group leaving the church, and 3) properly discipled, they have the greatest influence on their fellow students for

Christ than any other source. ES applies to students of all denominations, cultures, and ethnicities.

Multitudes of intermediate, high school, and college students are vulnerable to worldly temptations laced with immorality, addictive habits, and enticing entertainment that leads to eternal destruction and they do not have the spiritual foundation to cope with these distractions!

In the United States, adults are forbidden to go on campus and evangelize students but Christian students are not forbidden to express themselves! Thus, the way to return Christian influence into schools and out into the community is through discipled student peers.

Schools are supposed to prepare students for life. Yet school administrators and teachers are forbidden to prepare students for their eternal future!

How Sustained ES Networks Work:

Obedience Assignment: ☐

> 48. Contact couples that have completed EP and offer to prepare them to start a student discipleship movement

ES is a student discipleship ministry based upon the great commission, (Matthew 28:18-20). The ES process is the same as EP but focused on students rather than parents. Thus, an ES teacher that has completed EP should be prepared to teach ES to students.

Three Day ES Manager /Teacher /Coordinator Training:

Obedience Assignment: ☐

> 49. Secure ES binders for each couple that agrees to teach a small group of students.

ES manager / trainer / coordinator training can be self-taught from the material in this book and from the www. equipingstudents.com website.

More than one couple can be commissioned as ES manager trainers or coordinators for a region upon completion of the three-day training session. ES training should be accomplished in a home or at the training facility selected for discipling 4 to 6 students.

Evening of Day One ES Training: will be a brief overview of ES.

The managers need not perform all of the arrangements for the ES course but will seek help from other Christian adults and make sure that all arrangements are made in advance of the initial student instruction. EP is the best source for helpers.

Like EP, the ES teachers will be responsible for a suitable location to perform the student training.

The location should be off-campus unless arrangements can be coordinated with school administration for school facilities. This facility should have enough space for a class of 4 to 6 students along with several adults.

John and Dot Overton

Obedience Assignment: ☐

> 50. Arrange for a location to start a Discipleship course for up to six students.

The facility should have: 1) Electrical power and an extension cord with at least two outlets, 2) Tables for students to write on, 3) Individual chairs, 4) A screen, or suitable wall for projecting training slides, 5) Restrooms, and 6) Good lighting. Access to a quality copy machine will be very useful. A home, public building, or church may provide a suitable facility for ES training.

Each student that commits to this ES course should be supplied: 1) a study Bible, 2), a Student binder containing study manuals, lists of scriptures, ES forms and a journal, and 4) a quality writing pen. The estimated cost of these materials is indicated on the website. These materials may be downloaded free from the equipping students website or bound copies may be purchased from the website (Special Note: If the students prefer using their smart phones or tablets for their daily times with the Lord, then the Bibles and journals will not be needed. If a large quality screen TV with a USB port is available, the training projections may be generated from the thumb drive).

The teachers will schedule and conduct eight ES classes for the group of students. Adult coordinators will sit in these classes as monitor/helpers in preparation to equip another group of students in the future. The first class will be to establish transparent communication between the teachers and the students. The teachers will explain the purpose and scope of ES and ask for commitment to complete eight approximately one to one and a half hour classes as well as be accountable for accomplishing weekly goals to be set by the class. Each student must understand what is involved and agree to complete the course or be lovingly dismissed. Replacing any dropouts with additional students must be resisted. Students should not be added to the group after the first session. The teachers will share their relationship with Jesus and ask each student to tell about their relationship with Jesus. It is crucial that clear verbalization about personal relationships be expressed.

During the first class, each student will use form ES1 in their binder to write their story. Their story (their relationship with Jesus) must be brief and understandable by other students. They are then to write a bridge to the Gospel and recite John 3:16. The students selected for the group should be able to recite John 3:16 but the teachers should be prepared to help them memorize it if they are not. They are then to use Form ES2 to list the names of students they know that are away from God.

Like EP, a scripture-based vision will be cast and a brief discipleship lesson will be taught by the teacher during each ES session. A set of goals to be accomplished by the students and the ES teacher before the next meeting will be agreed upon. The students must understand that they will be accountable for reporting the results of their goals at the following meeting.

The inclination to recruit a large group of students must be resisted. By restricting the focus on a few selected students, a multiplying movement is much more likely to be sustained. Be sure to sign extra students up for future classes.

The ES managers will teach the initial eight-week ES course to the first student group. Near the completion of the first student course, the students will recommend a second group of four to six students for ES discipleship. The coordinators that monitored the first series of classes will teach the second group of students. A different student training location may be needed and student supplies secured before starting additional classes.

A network of adult teacher/coordinators will be recruited to monitor subsequent student classes and each student class will recommend additional groups of students to be equipped. Thus, ES will become a sustaining movement of Christian discipleship among students. These students will influence their peers, siblings, parents, and teachers to become followers of Christ.

Training, Basic ES Strategy, Day Two:

Today will be a full day of instruction on the ES process, along with a brief overview of the eight student equipping sessions. A mid-day break for lunch will be necessary.

Following opening prayer, remind the candidate managers /coordinators /trainers of the purpose of ES. Our commission is to build the kingdom: start locally (your schools) and move out to the uttermost parts of the world.

ES is for students that will be a part of a disciplship revolution. ES will only work if the managers/ teacher/ coordinators and the student group members commit themselves to faithfully obey selected New Testament commandments and commissions. They must be absolutely dependent upon the Holy Spirit to accomplish the objectives of ES.

The initial student sessions will be to equip each student with a Christian foundation. ES will then move the students from the classroom environment to share their faith in a laboratory like environment with other students. It is essential that the adult teachers lovingly share their Christian experiences with the students.

Each ES equipping session will include the same six parts taught in EP facilitated by an adult teacher, with occational student assistance.

Overview of the Eight Student Discipleship Sessions:

Student training materials for eight student sessions are on the thumb drive. Included are powerpoint outlines to be used by the teacher and manuals to be used by students to follow along with the projected powerpoint images. The training classes use the same eight topics taught for EP but tailored to students.

Training, Day Three, Field Training:

Today, the managers /teachers /coordinators will be taken through an ES laboratory where they will apply the ES tools and make sure they relate to what the group of students will be asked to do. Day 3 will start with breakfast in one of the manager / teacher homes or a private area of a restaurant.

During the course of their time together, the managers/ coordinators will write their story, prepare a bridge to the Gospel, memorize John 3:16, and prepare a list of adults that they know are away from God. They may be Christians or non-Christians.

The adults will share their story and recite John 3:16 like the students will be expected to do.

After breakfast, the adults will make contact with one of the people on their list and invite him/her to coffee or tea. The time together should be pleasant and unrushed. This should be a loving encounter with no pretense of trying to sell anything or talk them into anything.

During the conversations, tell your story as led by the Holy Spirit. Remember that this must be very brief and easy to understand.

Continue with your bridge to the Gospel.

Recite John 3:16 as the Gospel.

Ask if you can be of help to your friend. Agree to follow up with them at their convenience. Thank them for responding to your request to enjoy a cup of coffee and assure them that you will be praying for them. Give them a Christian tract and ask if they need a Bible. An appropriate tract is available on the thumb drive or from the website.

This part of manager training will be necessary to assure students that the managers have experienced all they will be asking the students to do.

Training, Evening of Day 3:

The managers/trainers/coordinators will meet during the evening to discuss ES, share questions they have, and problems they foresee. A time will be used to pray for students, parents, teachers, and their school campuses. Pray that ES will be anointed to start a sustained spiritual awakening among students.

A commissioning service will be conducted during which the managers, teachers, and coordinators will be recognized and commissioned with dated ES certificates.

Conclusion: You absolutely must raise the bar of expectation for your students. Just trying to build a crowd by feeding free pizza, playing games, and providing worldly entertainment is misleading your youth to think that such activity is all that Christianity is about. When they mature into adulthood, and the free stuff and entertainment is no longer offered, we lose them! What a tragedy!

Asking students to become disciples/equippers raises the bar of expectation radically! Jesus was a radical! These students are making final preparations for their lives. They will soon marry and become parents and bring new generations into the world. They will influence our culture economically, morally, and spiritually. The field is, indeed, ripe for harvest. Now is our only chance to guide them.

Jesus said, "I will build My Church; You Go, make disciples..."

Note: The ES managers /trainers /coordinators will need a laptop with Microsoft Power point and Microsoft Word, and a video projector to project the Power point training slides onto a screen or blank wall or access to a large screen TV with USB port.

Summary: If you are being led to co-labor with Jesus by becoming an ES manager to change the world, check out the free tools offered on the www.equippingstudents.com website.

Equipping Central (EC): EC located in Texas, USA, will oversee the ES ministry on a global basis and will maintain all information and materials needed by the local managers, teachers, and coordinators to conduct the ES process. This includes Power point slides, student manuals, and student forms. These materials may be printed from the thumb drive, downloaded from the ES website, or secured from Equipping Central. Communications between Equipping Central and the ES Managers will be by way of the Internet. Equipping Central will maintain an Equipping Students (ES) website and publish an ES newsletter. The ES managers, teachers, coordinators, and parent - student disciples will send messages and photographs of events to Equipping Central for inclusion in the newsletters and website.

Contact us by email at:
Pastor Bob Gibson
pastorbobatlsm@gmail.com
Or
John and Dot Overton at
dotnjohn@comcast.net

www.equippingstudents.com

ES FORMS:

Following are standard ES forms to be used for EP and ES discipleship training. Extra copies will need to be duplicated for distribution to each parent and student.

ES 1: My Story:
My Name: _____

_____

_____

_____

_____

My Bridge to the Gospel

_____

_____

_____

_____

The Gospel (John 3:16)

_____

_____

_____

_____

ES 2 — List of People I know that are Away from God

My Name:_____

Name	Cell Phone or email

1. _____

2. _____

3. _____

4. _____

5. _____

6. _____

7. _____

8. _____

ES 3 - List of others that are interested in becoming a Disciple of Christ and taking the EP or ES course

My Name:_____

Name   Cell Phone or email

1. _____

2. _____

3. _____

4. _____

5. _____

6. _____

7. _____

8. _____

ES 4 — Request to become an ES Manager

MyName: _____

Date: _____

Phone: _____

email: _____

Home Address: _____

Attending a Church? () **No, Yes** at:

_____

We are a married Christian couple making this request (Y), (N)

We are abiding Disciples of Christ practicing daily disciplines of prayer, and Bible study. (Y), (N)

I request to be certified as an ES Manager for the following: (City), (USA State), (Country)

_____

If selected, I agree to study the ES materials (including each student presentation), perform weekly goals, and be accountable to the group by reporting how I fulfilled my weekly goals.

_____

Signature

Comments about why I (we) should be selected:

About the Editor

Will Overton, John and Dot's grandson, is a Baylor University senior preparing to receive his Bachelor of Arts degree in Professional Writing

Printed in the United States
By Bookmasters